# UNICORN

## COLORING BOOK FOR KIDS

### Ages 4 - 6

## 86 pages and 8,5 x 11 in

## This book belongs to:

.....................................................................

.....................................................................

.....................................................................

This Unicorn Coloring Book is prepared especially for kids ages 4-6 so as they can enjoy these cute drawings.

This book contains 86 pages. There are enough pages for kids so as to get fun from this coloring activity , and also to learn how to color and follow the shapes of drawings.

As we know, kids love such activities and such creatures; that's why we prepared this kind of book so as to give them this chance and let them live great moments of happiness and fun.

So, if kids want to get enjoyment, happiness and fun; and if they want to improve their creativity and imagination, then this is the right book.

Please, if you have any remark about this book, do not hesitate to send us an email via:
apamog@hotmail.com

# Thank you.